FASHION SCIENCE

SCIENCE 24/7

ANIMAL SCIENCE

CAR SCIENCE

COMPUTER SCIENCE

ENVIRONMENTAL SCIENCE

FASHION SCIENCE

FOOD SCIENCE

HEALTH SCIENCE

MUSIC SCIENCE

PHOTO SCIENCE

SPORTS SCIENCE

TRAVEL SCIENCE

SCIENCE 24/7

FASHION SCIENCE

JANE P. GARDNER

SCIENCE CONSULTANT:
RUSS LEWIN
SCIENCE AND MATH EDUCATOR

Mason Crest

Mason Crest
450 Parkway Drive, Suite D
Broomall, PA 19008
www.masoncrest.com

Printed and bound in the United States of America.

Series ISBN: 978-1-4222-3404-4
Hardback ISBN: 978-1-4222-3409-9
EBook ISBN: 978-1-4222-8493-3

First printing
1 3 5 7 9 8 6 4 2

Produced by Shoreline Publishing Group LLC
Santa Barbara, California
www.shorelinepublishing.com
Cover photograph: Dreamstime.com/Wavebreakmedia Ltd.

Library of Congress Cataloging-in-Publication Data
Gardner, Jane P., author.
    Fashion science / by Jane P. Gardner ; science consultant, Russ Lewin, science and math educator.
    pages cm. -- (Science 24/7)
    Audience: Grades 9 to 12
    Includes bibliographical references and index.
ISBN 978-1-4222-3409-9 (hardback) -- ISBN 978-1-4222-3404-4 (series) -- ISBN 978-1-4222-8493-3 (ebook) 1. Fashion--Miscellanea--Juvenile literature. 2. Clothing and dress--Technological innovations--Juvenile literature. I. Title.
TT515.G37 2015
746.92--dc23
                                                                    2015005002

IMPORTANT NOTICE
The science experiments, activities, and information described in this publication are for educational use only. The publisher is not responsible for any direct, indirect, incidental or consequential damages as a result of the uses or misuses of the techniques and information within.

Contents

KEY ICONS TO LOOK FOR

Words to Understand: These words with their easy-to-understand definitions will increase the reader's understanding of the text, while building vocabulary skills.

Sidebars: This boxed material within the main text allows readers to build knowledge, gain insights, explore possibilities, and broaden their perspectives by weaving together additional information to provide realistic and holistic perspectives.

Series Glossary of Key Terms: This back-of-the-book glossary contains terminology used throughout this series. Words found here increase the reader's ability to read and comprehend higher-level books and articles in this field.

INTRODUCTION

Science. Ugh! Is this the class you have to sit through in order to get to the cafeteria for lunch? Or, yeah! This is my favorite class! Whether you look forward to science or dread it, you can't escape it. Science is all around us all the time.

What do you think of when you think about science? People in lab coats peering anxiously through microscopes while scribbling notes? Giant telescopes scanning the universe for signs of life? Submersibles trolling the dark, cold, and lonely world of the deepest ocean? Yes, these are all science and things that scientists do to learn more about our planet, outer space, and the human body. But we are all scientists. Even you.

Science is about asking questions. Why do I have to eat my vegetables? Why does the sun set in the west? Why do cats purr and dogs bark? Why am I warmer when I wear a black jacket than when I wear a white one? These are all great questions. And these questions can be the start of something big . . . the start of scientific discovery.

1. **Observe:** Ask questions. What do you see in the world around you that you don't understand? What do you wish you knew more about? Remember, there is always more than one solution to a problem. This is the starting point for scientists—and it can be the starting point for you, too!

Enrique took a slice of bread out of the package and discovered there was mold on it. "Again?" he complained. "This is the second time this all-natural bread I bought turned moldy before I could finish it. I wonder why."

2. **Research:** Find out what you can about the observation you have made. The more information you learn about your observation, the better you will understand which questions really need to be answered.

Enrique researched the term "all-natural" as it applied to his bread. He discovered that it meant that no preservatives were used. Some breads contain preservatives, which are used to "maintain freshness." Enrique wondered if it was the lack of preservatives that was allowing his bread to grow mold.

3. **Predict:** Consider what might happen if you were to design an experiment based on your research. What do you think you would find?

Enrique thought that maybe it was the lack of preservatives in his bread that was causing the mold. He predicted that bread containing preservatives would last longer than "all-natural" breads.

4. **Develop a Hypothesis:** A hypothesis is a possible answer or solution to a scientific problem. Sometimes, they are written as an "if-then" statement. For example, "If I get a good night's sleep, then I will do well on the test tomorrow." This is not a fact; there is no guarantee that the hypothesis is correct. But it is a statement that can be tested with an experiment. And then, if necessary, revised once the experiment has been done.

Enrique thinks that he knows what is going on. He figures that the preservatives in the bread are what keeps it from getting moldy. His working hypothesis is, "If bread contains preservatives, it will not grow mold." He is now ready to test his hypothesis.

5. **Design an Experiment:** An experiment is designed to test a hypothesis. It is important when designing an experiment to look at all the variables. Variables are the factors that will change in the experiment. Some variables will be independent—these won't change. Others are dependent and will change as the experiment progresses. A control is necessary, too. This is a constant throughout the experiment against which results can be compared.

Enrique plans his experiment. He chooses two slices of his bread, and two slices of the bread with preservatives. He uses a small kitchen scale to ensure that the slices are approximately the same weight. He places a slice of each on the windowsill where they will receive the same amount of sunlight. He places the other two slices in a dark cupboard. He checks on his bread every day for a week. He finds that his bread gets mold in both places while the bread with preservatives starts to grow a little mold in the sunshine but none in the cupboard.

6. **Revise the hypothesis:** Sometimes the result of your experiment will show that the original hypothesis is incorrect. That is okay! Science is all about taking risks, making mistakes, and learning from them. Rewriting a hypothesis after examining the data is what this is all about.

Enrique realized it may be more than the preservatives that prevents mold. Keeping the bread out of the sunlight and in a dark place will help preserve it, even without preservatives. He has decided to buy smaller quantities of bread now, and keep it in the cupboard.

This book has activities for you to try at the end of each chapter. They are meant to be fun, and teach you a little bit at the same time. Sometimes, you'll be asked to design your own experiment. Think back to Enrique's experience when you start designing your own. And remember—science is about being curious, being patient, and not being afraid of saying you made a mistake. There are always other experiments to be done!

1
SILK

Milena and her best friend, Nisha, were at their favorite thrift store, Xcetera. The store has a large selection of gently used clothing at prices that fit in with the girls' budgets. The store and its owner, Ms. Champi, sells some new clothing as well as used books and other items. Milena and Nisha go to the store often, as there is always new stuff to see.

Nisha rifled through a rack of colorful tops. "Oooh, I like this one. It's 100 percent silk, too."

Milena came over to take a look. She rubbed the material between her fingers, saying, "This is pretty. You do realize, don't you, that silk is basically worm spit."

Nisha stared at her in disbelief. "Worm spit? No way. I thought silk came from a plant, sort of like cotton."

Milena shook her head. "Nope. Sorry to have to be the one to tell you."

Nisha laughed. "Okay, then how does it happen? How do we get from worm spit to this awesome blouse?"

"I read something about the whole thing a while ago," Milena explained. "These special worms, called silkworms, make it. Silkworms go through their life cycle and eventually become silk moths. When they are caterpillars, they eat mulberry leaves and grow. The caterpillar spins a COCOON made of silk around its body. While inside the cocoon, the caterpillar turns into a PUPA. The pupa eventually becomes a moth and comes out of the cocoon. The moth will mate with other moths, lay eggs, which turn into caterpillars and the cycle continues."

"So, the silk comes from the cocoons?" asked Nisha.

"Yes. There are two glands on the top of the caterpillar's head. They release the silk from there and wrap themselves in the silk cocoon."

"And people then take the cocoons and remove the silk from them?" asked Nisha.

"I read that a single caterpillar can spin about a mile of silk thread in just a couple of days," said Milena. "That makes up their cocoon."

Words to Understand

COCOON a silky case spun by the larvae of many insects during one of its stages of development

PUPA a stage in the life cycle of some insects

The downside of using silkworm cocoons to make silk?
The cocoons are boiled . . . with the caterpillars inside.

"Wow! That's a busy caterpillar. What happens next?"

Milena continued. "This is where it gets a little tricky. The cocoons, pupa and all, are soaked in boiling water. This loosens the material holding the cocoon together. Then the cocoon is carefully unwound, hopefully leaving a long, unbroken thread."

Nisha looked at the cocoon, her eyes huge with disbelief. "You mean the caterpillar dies?"

"Yes. I told you this step was tricky. The caterpillar does die. That's how silk is made. It's been made like this for centuries."

Nisha rubbed the cloth between her fingers again. "This is so soft and beautiful. It's hard to imagine all that went into making it."

Peace Silk

While silk is a natural fiber, it does result in the death of thousands of silk worms. Many people are concerned with this practice and have turned to a product called "peace silk" as an alternative. Peace silk is made from the broken cocoons of silkworms that have emerged as silk moths. The threads of the broken cocoons are fixed together by spinning them. The resulting silk is thicker, softer, and more delicate than traditional silk. And it is more expensive as the process is more complex. Perhaps you can consider looking for products made of peace silk if you have concerns about the plight of the silkworms.

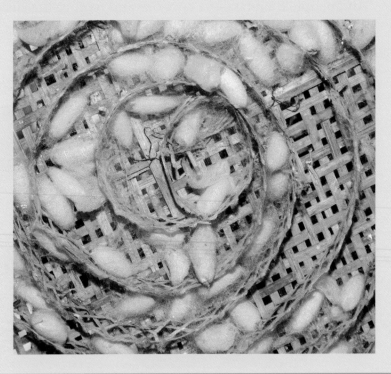

Try it Yourself

What is your clothing made of? It is made of a plant? Or worm spit? Or was it made in a lab? Have you ever wondered about it? Perhaps it is worth a closer look.

Materials:
- one article of clothing, with the tag
- Internet access
- poster board
- markers, pencils

1. Identify a piece of clothing you would like to investigate. It could be your favorite pair of jeans, a warm jacket, or a fashionable pair of basketball socks. Be sure that the clothing still has the tag attached inside telling what it is made of, or that you still have the original packaging.

2. What materials is it made of? Many items of clothing today are made of more than one type of fabric, and the relative percentages are usually listed.

3. Use the Internet to find out more about each of the fabrics in your clothing. Where was it made? How was it made? What products go into the fabric? Were there any surprises?

4. Share what you have learned with the world! Create a poster tracing the fabrics to your item of clothing. Discuss any environmental concerns that may be associated with the fabric. Would you buy this clothing again?

2
WEARABLE TECHNOLOGY

"Well, if it isn't two of my favorite students."

The girls looked up to see Mr. Rand, their science teacher, in front of a display of new jackets.

"Mr. Rand! You shop here?" Nisha and Milena were surprised to see him at Xcetera. They weren't used to seeing their teachers outside of school.

Mr. Rand smiled and said, "I sure do. There are so many good bargains here. And I know the owner, too."

"Oh, we know Ms. Champi too," said Milena. "She has the best eye for all this stuff."

"I actually help her out a bit, too. I have helped her bring in some of this wearable technology lately."

"Wearable technology? What's that?"

Mr. Rand picked up a bracelet from the counter. "What does this look like?"

"It looks like a bracelet or a watch but it's pretty plain," Nisha said.

Mr. Rand took out his phone and called up an app. He showed the girls the screen while pulling up his sleeve to show that he was wearing the same sort of bracelet. "This can track all sorts of things. It measures the number of steps I take each day, how far I traveled, and the number of calories I burn. It also helps track my sleep patterns."

Nisha stared at the bracelet. "It can do all that? How?"

"You have to personalize it. There is a lot of information you have to input—things like height, weight, age, and gender. The sensor in the bracelet then measures things like your heart rate and it calculates the different factors."

"That is pretty cool," Milena said. "What other kinds of wearable technology are there?"

"Well, there are monitors that doctors can give their patients. They keep track of things like

Fitness monitors measure body movements and transmit information wirelessly to an app to help people keep track of their exercise.

blood pressure or blood sugar levels. There have been many advances for athletes, too. High-tech clothing helps monitor their oxygen levels, for example, to maximize their workouts."

"And isn't there a lot that is done today with GPS systems in clothing and other things you can wear, to help hikers?" added Nisha.

"Yes, GPS locators are getting more and more sophisticated," said Mr. Rand. "And they are showing up everywhere."

Smart Clothes

New technology is being developed all the time. Clothing and accessories with GPS and sensors to monitor heart rate and oxygen are being developed for firefighters, police officers, and military personnel. This can help locate and monitor the status of these people as they work under some of the most difficult and dangerous of circumstances.

Try it Yourself

What would you invent for wearable technology if you could? What if you had no budget restraints and all the available technology at your fingertips? What would you dream up? Would you look to make clothing that could help people be healthy? Or transmit information about their vital signs to their doctor? Or make people more comfortable? What would you do?

Materials:
- Internet access
- pen and paper

1. It is the year 2030, and you work for a company that creates new clothing for the modern teenager. Your job is to design a new jacket that uses technology to improve or enhance the teenager's experience. What would you do?

2. Research available technology and brainstorm what you, as a teenager, would like to see. How would you implement this? Be creative.

3
COLORS
MATTER

"I could really use a new winter jacket," said Nisha. "My dad said if I could find one that was relatively cheap, that would be okay. He thinks I should wear the one I got last winter. But what does he know!?"

Milena held up a jacket from a nearby rack. "Here's a nice white one."

"No," said Nisha. "You can't wear a white jacket in the winter, especially if I want to wear it skiing."

Milena was surprised. "You are that concerned about the whole 'no white clothes after Labor Day' thing?"

Nisha picked out a black ski jacket. "No, that's an old rule. It used to be that women were not supposed to wear white clothes in the fall or winter. But there is actually a good reason not to wear white. White doesn't absorb as much heat as a darker jacket. So wearing a dark jacket will keep me warmer."

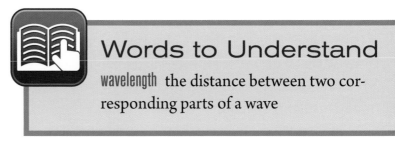

"Seriously?" Milena was skeptical. "The color of the jacket really has that much of an effect?"

Nisha looked a little less sure as she tried on the jacket. "Well . . . that's what I heard."

"Let's see if we can figure this out," Milena said. "What color is this jacket?" she asked, pointing to a different one on the rack.

"That's red."

"And why does it look red?"

Nisha caught on to what Milena was trying to explain. "It is red because when light hits it, all of the colors in the light are absorbed, except for red. The **wavelength** for red is reflected back to our eyes, and we see that."

"Yes, that's right!" Milena related what they had learned in science class. "And something that is white will reflect all the light back to our eyes. The wavelengths of colors are not absorbed."

Nisha finished her friend's thought. "Which means that if something looks black to us, then

Wavelengths of Light

The light we see, visible light, is electromagnetic radiation. All electromagnetic waves have different wavelengths and frequencies. Passing light through a prism separates it into its different wavelengths. Red light has the longest wavelength of all visible light; violet has the shortest.

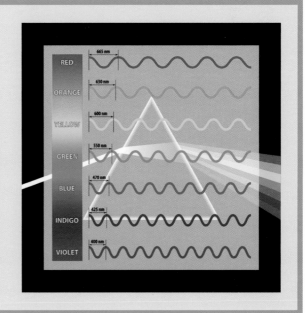

all of the wavelengths of light are absorbed along with the heat that light brings. So, wouldn't it make sense that a darker coat would keep you warmer than a lighter coat?"

Milena agreed. "I think so. If everything else was equal. I mean if they had the same sort of fabric and insulation of course, then I do believe the darker colored one would keep you warmer in the winter sunshine than a lighter colored one."

"Which is why . . ." Nisha pulled a dark blue ski jacket off the rack and continued, "I really like this one!"

This shows one way to set up the boxes for the experiment described on page 19.

Try it Yourself

Do dark colors really absorb more heat than light colors? Find out with this experiment using small boxes made of different colored paper, ice cubes, and some help from the sun! (sample of experiment at left)

Materials:

- four sheets of heavy-weight paper—white, yellow, red, and black
- scissors
- tape
- four ice cubes
- sunshine or heat lamp
- timer/stop watch
- paper towels

1. Make a prediction. Which color do you think will heat up the quickest? Why do you think this?

2. Use scissors and tape to construct four small boxes, one from each color paper. Leave one side open.

3. Place an ice cube in each of the boxes and lay them on their sides so that you can see in them and the ice is not in direct sunlight.

4. Shine the heat lamp on the boxes—or expose them one at a time to the sun's direct light—and time how long it takes for each ice cube to melt.

5. What did you find? Was your prediction correct?

4

TO WASH OR NOT TO WASH

Milena and Nisha moved over to a rack of denim jeans. "Look at this," Nisha said as she held up a faded pair. "The last owner actually wrote dates inside the jeans."

"Let me see," said Milena. "Ugh! You know what this is? I think those are the dates that the person washed these jeans." Milena looked at the tag in disbelief.

Nisha grabbed the jeans back from her. "Seriously? Look, they go for months, and even a year once, without washing them!"

Their science teacher Mr. Rand walked by at that moment. "Didn't you know that? You don't have to wash denim that often."

"What!? Why would someone do that? Do they want to lose all their friends?" Milena was horrified.

Mr. Rand smiled. "Actually, from what I read recently, raw denim lasts longer if you don't wash it."

"Really? I still don't get it." Nisha admitted.

Mr. Rand explained. "You know that worn-in look people like in their jeans? The longer you go without washing the dye off the denim, the more natural the worn-in look will be. Some people have gone months, and even years, without washing their jeans. They simply air them out on a clothes line or something to freshen them."

Nisha and Milena still had their doubts.

"And, if the perfectly worn and faded pair of jeans isn't enough," Mr. Rand explained, "then the fact that you would save considerable amounts of water each year might convince you."

He went on, "Older washing machines, the ones where you load the clothes in from the top, use an average of 40 gallons of water each load. The newer ones are usually better; they might use in the realm of 20 gallons of water per load. But it still adds up. Washing your jeans less frequently can have an impact."

Milena nodded. "I can see that. And there is the detergent you use and the energy to dry the jeans. I see what you mean, Mr. Rand. I just am not sure if I can do it."

Mr. Rand understood. "I get it. But at least you are aware of it. Perhaps you will change your mind someday, or make little changes. Little changes add up."

Jeans are among the most popular styles of clothing in the United States. In 2014, Americans bought more than $16 billion of jeans products.

Energy Star

The U.S. Environmental Protection Agency has a voluntary program called the Energy Star program. It was established in 1992 as part of the Clean Air Act. The Energy Star program is designed to save companies and individual families money in energy costs and to protect the environment at the same time. It encourages the promotion of energy-efficient products, which in turn results in lower energy use and a reduction in pollution. Appliances that meet these new standards are clearly labeled an Energy Star product.

Try it Yourself

Does washing denim really make it wear faster? Or differently? Try this experiment. You won't have to skip washing your jeans entirely, but who knows, you may end up changing your habits!

Materials:

- two squares, approximately 6"x 6" each, of unwashed raw denim
- safety pins
- washing machine and detergent

1. Find out what happens to denim when you don't wash it and compare that to denim that you do wash.

2. Pin one square of unwashed raw denim on each leg of another pair of pants you will wear with some regularity. Wear them as you normally would. When it is time to wash them, unpin one square while leaving the other square to run through the wash and dry cycle.

3. When dried, pin the other square back onto the pant leg. Examine both for any changes in color or feel.

4. What do you think you will find?

5. Continue the wash and wear cycle for several weeks or months.

6. How has this experience changed the way you look at washing denim?

5
A SENSE OF STYLE

Nisha held up a fuchsia sweater with bright orange trim. "So what do you think? Is this great or what?"

Milena stood back to take a good look. She glanced at her friend's sweater choice. "You're kidding, right? That is hideous."

"Really? I kinda like it." Nisha held it up to her body in front of the full-length mirror. "I think it looks good."

"Well, you'll certainly not have to worry about someone at school having the same one. Someone brought it to the thrift store on purpose, you know."

Mr. Rand overheard the girls and their conversation. "You know, girls," he said. "There is actually a scientific reason for your opinions."

Milena looked skeptical. "Scientific? Really?"

Mr. Rand laughed. "Yes, scientific."

Nisha had her doubts, too. "Why would scientists be interested in fashion?" She realized she was talking to her science teacher, so she backtracked. "I mean, not that scientists, or science teachers, aren't fashionable, but why would they spend money to study fashion?"

Mr. Rand laughed again. "Don't worry, Nisha. I'm not insulted! But I understand what you are saying. I thought the same thing at first when I read the study. But think about it. First impressions are huge, right?"

The girls both nodded.

"Decisions about whether or not a person is hired for a job, if someone is going to date another person, or if you are scared of someone else or not—those things are decided quickly. And a lot of that has to do with the way the person is dressed.

"And then I learned that fashion is a 1.7 *trillion*-dollar industry. I realized that perhaps scientists are on to something. There must be a science behind what is in fashion and looks good and what doesn't."

"So what did they look at?" Milena asked. "It seems like there are a lot of different things in fashion—style, color, length, accessories, and lots of other options."

"That's exactly right." Mr. Rand had their complete attention now. "The study I read looked at colors. And more specifically, the relationship between how well colors coordinate, or not, and whether or not they were considered to be fashionable."

Nisha reluctantly held up the sweater she was holding. "You mean, whether something like this is fashionable?"

"Yes. That is a good example."

"So what did they find? What's the connection?" asked Milena.

"It's actually not that surprising," Mr. Rand answered. "For example, what if I said I was going to wear this shirt … and this tie, to school tomorrow." He rifled through the racks and picked out a brown shirt and a tie that was the same shade of brown.

"Ugh. Too much brown."

"What if I wore this." He held up a pair of dark grey slacks, a red shirt, a dark grey jacket, and a red belt.

Nisha looked at it and said, "Well, that is better than the brown outfit."

"Yes, but it looks like you tried too hard to match," added Milena.

"Okay, one more." Mr. Rand came back with a red plaid shirt and an oversized polka dotted suit coat.

Goldilocks

The science behind understanding what colors or patterns look best together is referred to sometimes as the Goldilocks Principle. Remember that Goldilocks entered into the home of the three bears and complained when things were either too hot or too cold and was only content when everything was "just right." The same applies to fashion sense apparently. It turns out that when it comes to fashion, too many clashing colors and patterns are as bad as too many matching colors. The "just right" in fashion is somewhere in between.

"Okay, now you are just being extreme, Mr. R," Nisha said. "No one would do that."

Mr. Rand looked at the clothes in his hand. "Okay, maybe you are right. But I made my point, didn't I?"

Milena looked at him unsurely. "Um . . . what was the point?"

Mr. Rand smiled and said, "Those extremes are not what we consider to be attractive or fashionable. Overmatching, overplanning, and overpatterning is not the norm [an example at right!]. Scientists found that more average combinations of colors and patterns are more attractive to most people than wild combinations."

Nisha looked back at the sweater she found and said, "Well, I still say that this sweater is great. I love it. And I'm going to get it. It is within my boundary of acceptable colors, I guess."

"Good for you, Nisha. It's good to be bold sometimes," Mr. Rand said.

Try it Yourself

Do you have an eye for fashion and colors? What do you think is fashionable? What color combinations do you find suitable? If you were to design an outfit, what would you use?

Materials:
- scissors
- poster board
- glue
- markers
- fashion magazines and newspaper inserts

1. Make a poster of new fashion combinations. Use photographs and advertisements from magazines and newspaper ads.

2. Include outfits that are pleasing to the eye as well as those that clash.

3. Try to find new patterns and combinations that work for you.

4. Share your creations with your friends and get their opinions as well.

6

A UNIQUE
WATER FILTER

"Hey, Milena, look at this," Nisha called out as she stood in front of a display of women in brightly colored saris along the banks of a river. "These women live in Bangladesh and they are making filters out of their cotton saris."

"Let me see." Milena came over to the display. "It says they are fighting cholera. What is that?"

Nisha knew because she had done a report on waterborne diseases a few months before in science class. "It's a horrible disease that people get from drinking water that is contaminated. Cholera causes severe diarrhea, which can lead to dehydration and sometimes death. Poor sanitation is the main cause and also the way it spreads. Areas of Africa, Asia, and South America still have many, many cases of cholera each year."

"Yikes. Then this invention that these women have is a good thing?"

"Sounds like it. So what do they do?"

Words to Understand

cholera a highly infectious disease caused by a contaminated water supply or poor sanitation

Milena read more from the display. "These women discovered that by folding their saris a couple of times and then passing their drinking water through it, they could make a filter that would trap the bacteria that causes cholera. Oh, and this is pretty neat. Old saris make the best filters. Years of washing and wear help shrink the spaces in the fibers. Used cloth makes better filters."

Nisha pointed to the sign. "Actually, they have to fold the saris *four* times, at least, and they catch the plankton in the water that the bacteria holds on to."

"It looks as if these simple filters can catch upwards of 99 percent of the bacteria that cause cholera," Milena said. "That is huge. It is pretty impressive that such a simple filter can make such a significant difference in the lives of the people there."

Creative use of clothing helps prevent illness from tainted water.

Cholera

Cholera is an infection of the small intestine. It is caused by a bacterium spread from contaminated water or food. Most people who get cholera have severe diarrhea and vomiting, which can lead to dehydration. In 2010, there were an estimated 100,000–130,000 deaths from cholera. Most cholera deaths are in regions with poor sanitation facilities. The bacteria are most harmful to the elderly, children, and people with a lower immune system.

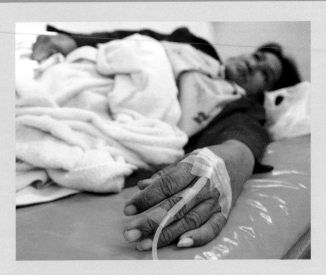

Try it Yourself

Could you make a filter that could clean water? What materials would you want to use? Design your own filter and test it.

Caution. Do not drink the water, even after you filter it. It will still be dirty and not fit for drinking.

Materials:

- liter soda bottle
- scissors
- coffee filters
- paper towels
- pieces of cloth
- water

- soil or sand
- beaker

1. Make a beaker of "contaminated" water. Add soil or sand to tap water and mix to make a cloudy mixture.

2. Create a funnel. Carefully cut the top third of a soda bottle off. Turn it upside down and place it back into the bottle, with the spout pointing down.

3. Make a filter out of coffee filters and place it in the funnel.

4. Pour part of the "contaminated" water into the filter. Watch and observe the passage of the water.

5. Did the water flow easily through the filter? How does the filtered water compare with the original water?

6. If necessary, repeat after adding more coffee liners to the filter.

7. How many coffee liners did you have to use to get clean water out of the filter? How clean was it compared with the original?

8. Unfold the coffee liners. What did they look like?

CALIFORNIA KING SHEET SET

CARILOHA

EXTRA DEEP POCKETS • HYPO-ALLERGENIC • ANTIBACTERIAL • ECO-FRIENDLY

SOFTEST BEDDING ON THE PLANET

100% VISCOSE
MADE FROM BAMBOO

7

ECO-FRIENDLY FASHION

"**M**ilena, feel these socks." Nisha held out a bright blue pair of socks to her friend.

"Those are pretty soft. What are they made of?"

Nisha smiled at her and said, "You won't believe it. But they are made of bamboo!"

"Bamboo? As in the same plant as that one on the counter?" Ms. Champi had a decorative bamboo plant on the counter. There were several green stalks of the thin plant sticking out of a vase of water. "How is that possible? Why is it so soft?" Milena asked.

"I am not sure. But it is soft. Wait, look . . . here is a card that describes a bit about this kind of fabric."

Milena picked up a pair of the socks herself and read along. "Oh, this is a very sustainable fabric."

"What does that mean?" Nisha wondered.

"Hmmm. It says here that bamboo is the fastest-growing woody plant in the world. Some of the varieties of the plant can grow three feet (one meter) in just one day!"

"Wow. And look at this," Nisha said, pointing to the card. "Bamboo is one of the most environmentally friendly products out there. It's part of the grass family, so when it is harvested, it grows back without needing to replant new plants."

"And it doesn't take up much space either," added Milena. "Look at this; you can grow twice as much bamboo in the same area as you can cotton. There isn't a lot that has to be done to take care of bamboo either."

Mr. Rand passed by and overheard what the girls were talking about. "Did you know," he chimed in "that to make enough cotton for a pair of jeans and one tee shirt more than five thousand gallons (20,000 liters) of water must be used?"

"What!?" Nisha and Milena said together.

"Much of the world's cotton is grown in China, India, Pakistan, Uzbekistan, West Africa, and the United States. The pesticides used on cotton crops make up 24 percent of all pesticides sold in the entire world. Studies have shown that this has a negative impact not only on the environment but on the health of the workers in the cotton fields."

"Compare that to bamboo." Mr. Rand continued, "You have already mentioned some of the benefits to growing bamboo. There are others, too. Bamboo forests are useful in managing the watershed. They help control the quality of water. And prevent soil erosion. The roots

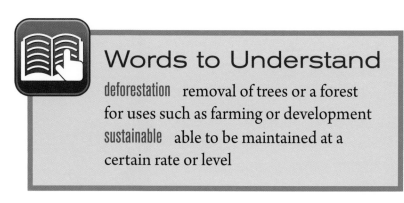

Words to Understand

deforestation   removal of trees or a forest for uses such as farming or development

sustainable   able to be maintained at a certain rate or level

of a bamboo plant are extensive and spread out, holding the soil in place. Forests of bamboo plants also keep evaporation of rivers and streams to a minimum with their large canopy. The canopy reduces the amount of sunlight that reaches the ground, reducing evaporation."

"This is sounding better and better," Nisha admitted. "And here is one more thing that makes me want to buy these socks. You know how we learned about greenhouse gases in science?"

Milena nodded. "Yeah. Plants take carbon dioxide out of the atmosphere. They take in carbon dioxide and use water and energy from the sun to make sugar and oxygen. That's photosynthesis. Mr. Rand jumped in. "Studies in Japan have shown that bamboo could potentially play a role in stabilizing the atmosphere. Roughly a half acre of bamboo will absorb as much as 12 tons of carbon dioxide from the air each year during photosynthesis. In return, these plants produce nearly 35 percent more oxygen than other trees. This exchange of carbon dioxide for oxygen can go a long way toward reducing the greenhouse gases in our atmosphere."

Milena continued, "Deforestation contributes to increasing levels of carbon dioxide in the atmosphere as the trees are cut down. So planting forests of bamboo can only help reverse that problem."

Nisha grabbed the socks off the rack. "I'm buying these. And I'm going to go find out what else is made of bamboo!"

Bamboo in Building

Over the past decade or so, bamboo flooring has become the most common use of this resource in construction in North America. Bamboo flooring is attractive to many for several reasons. Bamboo has fewer knots than other hardwoods, which many homeowners like. The wood is sustainable, making it environmentally friendly. Bamboo is durable, meaning it will withstand many of the nicks and scrapes that can mar softer flooring options. And it is less expensive than some other flooring options such as walnut or pine.

Try it Yourself

How fast does bamboo grow? Try it yourself and find out.

Materials:
- small bamboo plant
- fertilizer
- tape measure
- pen and paper
- graph paper or computer graphing program
- water

1. Purchase a small bamboo plant at your local nursery or supermarket. Make some initial measurements. Record information such as the diameter of the stalks and the height of the plant.

2. Carefully read the instructions on the care of your bamboo plant. Take note of how much it should be watered, whether or not it needs direct sunlight, and the fertilizers it might need. Do your best to support and grow your plant over a few months.

3. On a weekly basis, take measurements of the plant. Plot the changes in height and diameter over time.

4. How quickly does the plant grow in height? In diameter? What changes do you notice in the plant as it grows?

8
PRACTICAL FASHION

Nisha stopped to look at the books for sale in the store while Milena paid for her purchases. Nisha found a book about Sir Edmund Hillary and his climb with Tenzing Norgay up Mount Everest in 1953. She found the pictures in the book amazing, especially when she stopped to look closely at the clothing the men wore on their historic trip.

"Geez, Milena, look at this," she said.

Milena carried her two bags of clothes over to the bookshelves. "What is it?"

"This is a great book. It's all about the first two men to climb Mount Everest. But the weird thing is their clothes. Look at what they wore!"

Together, the girls looked at the photographs in the book. Hillary and Norgay both wore what looked to be simple snow pants and jackets. Many of the clothes looked to be made of wool. Their hats were thin under their bulky hoods and their boots looked clunky and awkward.

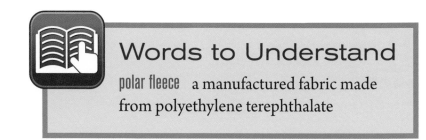
"I don't know," Nisha said. "Those clothes look like they would get wet and not really keep the wind out."

Milena was looking at the other books. "Here's a book about a more recent Everest climb. This one was in 1996."

This time, the girls saw hikers in brightly colored jackets and snow pants made of **polar fleece** and Gore-Tex and other modern-day materials. "This clothing looks like it would stay dry and keep out the wind."

"But I know that wool is a very warm fabric," said Nisha. "Perhaps Hillary wasn't that cold."

"I'm not sure," replied Milena. "I think there have been a lot of advances in the world of outdoor clothing since then. I mean, just look at the materials these climbers are wearing. The newer clothing seems to be lighter and less bulky. I bet it is more waterproof too."

Nisha nodded "Waterproofing is very important. When it comes to exerting yourself in a cold environment, it's so important to stay dry—inside and out."

The co-conqueror of Everest: Sir Edmund Hillary

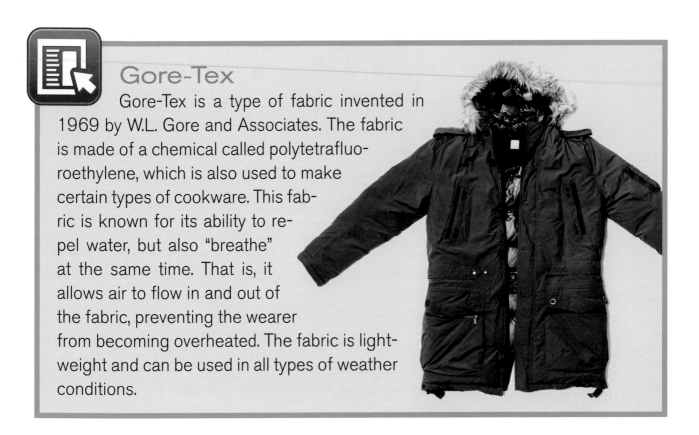

Gore-Tex

Gore-Tex is a type of fabric invented in 1969 by W.L. Gore and Associates. The fabric is made of a chemical called polytetrafluoroethylene, which is also used to make certain types of cookware. This fabric is known for its ability to repel water, but also "breathe" at the same time. That is, it allows air to flow in and out of the fabric, preventing the wearer from becoming overheated. The fabric is lightweight and can be used in all types of weather conditions.

"Inside and out? What do you mean?"

"I did some reading on this as I am thinking about joining the ski club this winter. It is recommended that you dress in layers to keep warm in the extreme cold. A layer of wicking material should be your base layer. Wicking material takes the moisture away from your skin. Moisture on your skin can make you feel cold. Cover this layer with some sort of breathable material. This lets the moisture pass through. You don't want to sweat and have that water vapor stuck close to your body. Breathable, wicking material is key. It will help keep you dry, and therefore warm, on the inside close to your body."

Milena interrupted. "But what about the waterproof stuff?"

Nisha continued, "The outer layer should be waterproof. To keep the snow and rain from the outside from coming in to get your body wet."

"That makes a lot of sense. I hope Hillary and the early adventurers like him had that information." Milena stared at the pictures and involuntarily shuddered. "You know, it is amazing to think about how science has played a role in so many things about clothing. I can imagine that Sir Edmund Hillary would have really liked to have had a pair of these high-tech boots for his trek up the mountain."

Try it Yourself

Which material would better withstand the cold and wet conditions on top of a mountain? Find out for yourself.

Materials:
- wool hat or scarf
- fleece hat or scarf
- two plastic cups, with lid
- thermometers
- hot tap water

1. Soak both of the hats or scarves in room temperature tap water. Wring them out so that they are still damp but not dripping.

2. Carefully place a plastic cup inside each. Fold down the top so you can access the cup easily.

3. Pour hot tap water into each cup and carefully place the top on them. Insert a thermometer through the hole for the straw in each one.

4. Unroll the hat or scarf so that it covers the top of the cup, but make sure you can still read the thermometer.

5. Measure the temperature of each container. Then, measure the temperature in each container every five minutes for at least 20 minutes.

6. What did you find?

7. What does this say about wool? Does it keep you warm even when wet?

9
CONCLUSION

Fashion Science. These are two words that are not typically thought of in the same sentence. But as you have seen, there is actually a lot of overlap between these two. Science plays a role in how we look at clothes, how clothes are made, and how they are cared for.

As with so many things in our lives today, the desire to be eco-friendly and create a sustainable world is important. Choices that we make as we choose the types of clothing we buy, how we care for them, and what this means for the environment are choices we need to make every day.

As Milena and Nisha found, there are fabrics out there that are more sustainable than others. There are materials used in our clothing that can help or harm the environment. This is important to keep in mind. Choosing to shop at a vintage or consignment store like they did is eco-friendly too.

Clothing is changing. Technology is becoming more and more a part of our everyday lives, and is even finding its way into what we wear. New materials are developed that protect us from ultraviolet radiation, from extreme cold, and from strong winds. Watch for more advances in the near future—especially in the areas of health care, health monitoring, and safety clothing.

There is one last activity for you to try. There are many laundry detergents and fabric softeners on the market today. And there is a lot of information about the dangers of some of the chemicals found in some of the common brands. Chemicals such as diethaolamine, benzaldehyde, and types of acid are found in detergents and fabric softeners. These scary sounding ingredients have been shown to cause irritation to the mouth, eyes, skin, and throat, rashes, and asthmatic symptoms. New products are showing up on shelves that do not contain these potentially harmful ingredients. But do they clean as well?

Take a few old clothes. Perhaps use a couple of old pillow cases, or some T-shirts you no longer wear. Get them dirty. Make a variety of stains—use ketchup, and mud, and marker for example. Design an experiment where you wash one dirty T-shirt in detergent containing some of the harmful ingredients, and one T-shirt in the environmentally friendly detergent. Be sure

Getting clothes clean can sometimes make the environment dirty.
Your choice of detergent could help make a difference.

to check the labels. What do you think will happen? What does happen? How do the detergents measure up? What do you think? Can you be clean and environmentally safe? What are the trade-offs, if any? How do you feel about how science has changed the way we do something as simple as wash our clothes. Share what you find out with your family and friends. Small changes can make a big difference!

Interested in fashion? You might consider a career in science. There could be a connection there for you!

This fashion designer's ideas start in his head and move to the paper. From there, they will need science to become reality.

Fashion Science 24–7: Concept Review

Chapter 1

Milena and Nisha find out how silkworms create the cocoons that are later turned into silk to make clothing.

Chapter 2

Technology to wear? Computers, apps, and devices are connecting what people wear to what people do in their daily lives, often to help with fitness goals.

Chapter 3

Colors of clothing matter for reasons other than style. Milena and Nisha learn that the color choices we make in clothes can affect our comfort.

Chapter 4

Milena and Nisha debate whether or not to wash jeans, by looking at the question from an energy-use point of view.

Chapter 5

The colors we wear can have an effect on other people—and us. Milena, Nisha, and Mr. Rand talk about the impact of our color and pattern choices.

Chapter 6

Milena and Nisha explore how cloth can literally save lives by acting as a water filter for people with access only to dirty water.

Chapter 7

Can we help save the world by the choices we make in clothing and bedding? Milena and Nisha find that bamboo might be the answer.

Chapter 8

Science has radically changed clothing worn to keep warm in cold weather. Milena and Nisha find out just how big the change has been.

FIND OUT MORE

Books

Do you realize all the inventions you use every day? There are tons. And a lot of them are associated with the clothes you wear. Check them out here.
Waxman, Laura Hamilton. *Fabulous Fashion Inventions (Awesome Inventions You Use Every Day)*. Minneapolis, Minn.: Lerner, 2013.

Want to be more eco-friendly when it comes to choosing your clothes? Read this guide for some helpful hints:
Gogerly, Liz. *A Teen Guide to Eco-Fashion*. New York: Heinemann, 2013.

Did the chapter about washing your blue jeans get you thinking? Want to know a little bit more about denim and the history of jeans? Try this book!
Kyi, Tanya. *The Blue Jean Book: The Story Behind the Seams*. Toronto.: Annick Press, 2005.

Web Sites

The production of silk, or sericulture, has a long history in China. Find out more about the history of silk and the Silk Road at this Web site:
www.silk-road.com/artl/silkhistory.shtml

How does it happen? How is worm spit turned into silk? Watch this video to find out.
www.sciencechannel.com/tv-shows/how-do-they-do-it/videos/how-do-they-do-it-silk-from-worm-spit.htm

Compare the equipment and clothing worn by Sir Edmund Hillary and modern day Mount Everest adventurers at this Web site:
adventure.nationalgeographic.com/adventure/everest/gear-edmund-hillary-hilaree-oneill/

Series Glossary of Key Terms

alleles different forms of a gene; offspring inherit one allele from each parent

chromosomes molecules within an organism that contain DNA

climate change the ongoing process in which the temperature of the Earth is growing over time

force in science, strength or energy that comes as a result of a physical movement or action

frequency number of waves that pass a given point in a certain period of time

friction the resistance encountered when an object rubs against another object or on a surface

gene molecular unit of heredity of living organisms

gravity the force that pulls objects toward the ground

greenhouse gases gases in the atmosphere that trap radiation from the sun

inertia tendency of an object to resist change in motion

laser an intensified beam of light

lift the force that acts to raise a wing or an airfoil

momentum the amount of motion by a moving object

semiconductor a substance that has a conductivity between that of an insulator and that of most metals

sustainable able to be maintained at a certain rate or level

traits characteristics of an organism that are passed to the next generation

wavelength a measurement of light that is the distance from the top of one wave to the next

Picture Credits

Dollarphoto:
  Nito 14
  Kurhan 21
  Elena Korn: 41

Dreamstime.com:
  Swisshippo 8
  Geargodz 9
  Markrhiggins 10
  Martinmark 12, 16
  Milagli 17
  Maonakub 20
  Justmeyo 24
  Razoomgames 26
  Yurasova 28
  Anwar Huq 29
  Dotocfoto 30
  Pilens 32
  Ddnyddny 34
  Photographerlondon 36
  Stockysnapper 38
  Bialasiewicz 40
  Wavebreakmedia 42

Nike/Pete Parkes: 13
Tim of Kingsland: 37

ABOUT THE AUTHOR

Jane P. Gardner has written more than a dozen books for young and young-adult readers on science and other nonfiction topics. She became an author after a career as a science educator. She lives in Massachusetts with her husband, two sons, plus a cat and a gecko!

ABOUT THE CONSULTANT

Russ Lewin has taught physics, robotics, astronomy, and math at Santa Barbara Middle School in California for more than 25 years. His creative and popular classes and curriculum include a hands-on approach to learning and exploring that instills a love of science in his students.

INDEX